# Much With Body

*i.m. Dorothy Wordsworth (1771-1855)*
*and for all those who live with pain*

# Much With Body

*Polly Atkin*

Seren is the book imprint of
Poetry Wales Press Ltd.
Suite 6, 4 Derwen Road, Bridgend, Wales, CF31 1LH
www.serenbooks.com
facebook.com/SerenBooks
twitter@SerenBooks

The right of Polly Atkin to be identified as
the author of this work has been asserted in accordance
with the Copyright, Designs and Patents Act, 1988.

ISBN: 978-1-78172-645-7
ebook: 978-1-78172-646-4

A CIP record for this title is available from the British Library.

The publisher acknowledges the financial assistance of the Books Council of Wales.

Cover artwork: 'Hiatus' by Nancy Farmer.
waterdrawn.com

Printed in Bembo by Severn, Gloucester.

# Contents

# Full Wolf Moon

*(Grasmere, January 2020)*

Everyone everywhere is talking about the moon.
The full wolf moon, supersized with probability,

the new year eclipse. Eclipsed.

We have no moon here, only rain
rain coming out of a sodden dark

a bristly dark scattered with rain drops

rain drops as stars. The matted pelt
of the wolf night the wolf sky the wolf clouds

no wolf no moon / no moon no wolf

that's how it works in the films and the books.
The sky concurs, growls far back

at the year as it crouches at the edge of the clearing

creeps forward on its haunches, low in the bracken,
ready to take us down.

# Hunting the Stag

The stag doesn't visit because you want him to. It doesn't work like that.
He doesn't materialise when you go out to look for him
with the good camera this time, coiled around your neck
and your sheepskin hat with the ears flaps on.
He does not trot down from the hill to greet you, tamed by your need.
He has his own matters to attend to. What did you expect?
You know what you become when you're like this. Too much, too much.
Scanning for movement in the undergrowth, beady and atavistic.
When you press your palm on the stone gate post and wish your wish
is selfish. The heron passes asking *what are you missing when you only look
for big things?* A selfish wish never comes good.

He is higher than you can walk today, or deeper.
You cannot make him come to you.
Not the great stag with his rustling mane not even
the small roe with his sapling antlers.

He will be standing in the shadow of the side street when you lock
up the shop. He will be standing in the shadow of the house
when you stay out too long, talking on the path through the trees
about loss till the fells dissolve into dusk and push you down to him.
You will feel him before you hear him.
You will hear him before you see him.
He will seem to step out of the walls of your house
or through them. You will think he is waiting for you
but you are incidental. He will go
to a place you haven't worked for years,
wade into the lake, bristling as swans
ripple out from his image. Don't want so much.

Come down from the woods. Empty your pockets
of pinecones and sticks. Light the fire. It doesn't work like that.
Light the candles. Nothing does.

# Fell

The stars come back in the early morning,
in the half light. Corrupted by the rain.
They look for a moment through the broken window
like the fells themselves, just where they should be, with that
rectangular look of theirs, that air of miniature.

A fallen city from a long dead people.

A tumbled henge. Shackles risen.

I am new in my body, suddenly storied.
The idea of asterism mapped onto asterism.
Visually obvious. Distinct in the season.
Ludicrous, unrepeatable myth.

# Isolation Blessing

It's like a sick month. I only travel
between the bedroom and living room, living room
and bathroom, bathroom and kitchen, kitchen
and garden. Only when essential or medical.
Each afternoon I put outside clothes on
and walk up the lane. I visit the heron.
The heron is displeased with proximity, pretends
not to be in, frozen amongst
the horsehair or stalking behind the rhododendrons.

I look for frogs in the drying pond.
I rest on mossy stones and logs,
unafraid of punishment for moving wrongly
beyond my own body's, here where only
the deer are watching, though once a police van
passes as I stand in a clearing, fixed
by the stare of a doe, and I reach for my waterbottle
as proof I am mobile / local / legal.

The centre of the village is as distant as the past
and as sad and shamed with danger. I do not
go there. I forget the ways. Some nights
as I sit in my chair before bed far places
sidle close, calling like owls
at the window, and the shrivelled globe bubbles up
like the loaf proving by the radiator and sings

in my living room, sings in my garden, sings
as I swim in the training pool of the bath.
We sing along, our voices a portal,
a path we walk alone together.
It is Easter. I don't believe in the stone
rolling back from the mouth of the tomb, but I do
believe in this – when we offer a blessing
to the birds and the birds sing back.

# Bluebell Season

This is what you wanted, isn't it? everything bluebells and you
giddy with it – dunking your face in the swell of them
in the late light

the cuckoo concealed on the common,
the wrens in the bracken, the ravens on the crag
impersonating

the trees talking to you, telling you how much it means to them
to be waving their limbs in the high sun, ecstatic,
the deer in the small copse staring up at you drunk with it

as you trot back down to your human life.
You're thinking about yourself divested of the self again you do it
often, putting yourself in second person.

What you mean is I
I wanted it, this bluebell high, the deer transfixed by my human body
unable to move forward, or backward, until I remove it

and its history.
You wanted out of it, this alarming body, its scent of harm.
You carry it home all the same.

# Photograph of an owl

there's an owl flying through this

you have to know it's there to see it

to pick it out, there, against the stone,

starting to rise to the trees on the ridge –

it began at one corner of the shown universe

startled from its dayhunt dayhaunt

by our casual voices

our footsteps crunch crunch

on the sun-dried bracken –

impossible to walk quietly this month on this earth

sick and dehydrated –

jolted into presence

a blurred tawny scrawl

across fragrant blue fellside

across grey crag speckled

with luminous lichen

silent its silence

giving it up –

only owl is so there and so not –

huge and unhearable

unmistakable and unlocatable

feather fleck or lichen

flying through this

and out

# Frog Season

You have been hunched on the sofa all evening, trying
to drag something up, to force it to manifest

in the dark, take shape out of shadows

it's not what you think     it never is, is it?

when you get up to fill & boil the kettle
you're caught in the hall     the carpet splits

into legs, striped flanks, that tiny brilliant
wriggling symbol
                              your heart leaps up

one by the front door, on the way in

                              you make your drink

one by the back door, on the way out

you gather each as you find it     distinguished
by movement     release them out of the door

they seem closest to achieving

you are saving them or thwarting them
you need to understand how their world is mapped

alone in the house, and the first two-frog night of summer

the heat has passed     you lay the duvet back on the bed

you declare Frog Season     heralded by the rain,
the closing of the school gates, the gurgling drains

when you regain your post, you've a new sense of purpose

a tiny moth circles the halo of the lamp

you wait for the rest to arrive

# Lakeclean

Still damp hours after I sank myself under the surface my hair
smells like violets when I run my hand through it

not the ones crushed at the edge of the path through the wood,
yesterday's shampoo. My skin smells of heat and mud.

I don't swim because it's challenging I swim because I can. For the body
released from the tyranny of gravity, resistance of air. Land

is the enemy. We are comfortable here, suspended, above,
in, and under. We dwell in transparency.

We sweep mountains aside with our arms without wincing.
We move with something like ease.

# Pond life

Each night before bed I check for frogs.
I count frogs to bring myself to the limits of sleep
or mammalian life. To stand apart
or together. Two at the threshold. One
perched on a blue plastic bag by the garden
door. One muddying the dark
between his legs as I launch one out
into the flowerbed. One wriggling round
the hinge of the front door as he opens it for
the one still tickling in my hands. Two
hopping in opposite directions in the hall.
One trying to phase to spectral in the bathroom.

Soon enough the passing of weeks
is measured by size of frog. When one
apparates by the cupboard solid
enough to hold tight in one hand without crushing
or wiggling through I think *pond life*
*is complete*. But more sprout out of the skirting,
flimsy as pinkie fingernails, flinging
their camouflaged bodies at our feet. Pond life
is forever. Pond life is ours. The carpet
wavers in the dim pond light like water
thickened by movement and weeds.

# Wrack of Summer

All along the lake shore the brambles
are coming ripe, swelling, shiny

compound eyes as traffic mirrors.
In the water red beech leaves turn

with each wave. Light ticks away
disguised as wasp drone. The fringes are fraying.

Red leaves in the water. Brown leaves on the shore.
The wrack of summer.

The trees are still full of it. Bracken
high and green. It feels like a trick

if you expect one thing
to not be so much like another.

In the water I drift. Red leaf
pretending I could still be green.

A damselfly, May-blue, skims by.
We are all as confused as each other.

If we stop moving, we come to ground.
Brown leaves on grey stones. The wrack

of summer. All along the lake road
things dying, or coming into their own.

# Habitats

We chase tiny frogs around the bathroom we chase
tiny frogs around the hall, invisible
on the Sludge Green carpet in the rainy gloom
invisible in the living room on Rental Brown.
This house is designed for tiny frogs to hide in
but not to survive in. We wake to find
dried tiny frogs curled around hot water pipes,
perfectly preserved and even smaller.
Tiny frogs are everywhere.
We cannot put down our feet. We float
above them like lilies, opening and closing
with the light, casting our shadows deep.
And tiny toads are trying to follow
where tiny frogs slither with ease, trying
to squeeze their awkward bodies under
the front door, where a dog once chewed
and scratched in desperate abandonment, carving
a sliver of a portal. Tiny toads are not agile.
They move as though dragging always through mud.
When I open the door to release a tiny
frog from the cave of my hand in the morning:
a row of tiny toads upturned
in a split in the wood on the doorstep, stuck.
I think they are dead till I flip them over.
They come back to life, but the life is feeble.
Tiny frogs hop in your hand, work through.
Tiny toads sit in your palm's valley, blinking.
Tiny frogs are always moving.
Tiny toads are always watching
waiting for the moment your primordial shudder
turns to Kindchenschema. In August
a tiny toad follows me into the lake
and I think that the lesson is over, but then
more tiny toads more tiny frogs
invisible on the Sludge Green invisible on the Brown.
We keep letting them out. We keep trying to save them.
But this is their truth. We are floundering. We have sunk
to the reeds at the bottom of a forgotten pond
we call home, a necropolis of tiny toad ghosts.

# Dark Hedges/Barbed Wire

Dark hedges are oozing, weeping spikes of rust
    twists of rust push through their skin like thorns
as though the beeches were not beeches but roses
    as though the beeches were not beeches but lions, iron
barbs through their skin, as though the beeches were martyrs,
    torsos trussed in metal, barbs through their skin, steel rope
cutting into their skin, concentric rings of garottes
    by which to age them. This is a slow dominance.

Dark hedges have been pinned down as though possessed as though
    a risk as though sacrificial. They bulge out grossly. Decade by decade
consume their chains, swallow them into themselves, push themselves out
    around them, flesh frothing over the wire as if round a strap.
They stand heavier now. They will not be hemmed in.
    I thought they were like me, sick with invasion, rust in our sap
leaking through each crack, everyone watching saying *don't you look well.*
    They visualise their bark as mud on the road,
the wire sinking into their reflection and dissolving.

    I have come as a tourist to admire the lines, the beauty where nature
meets husbandry. A row of beeches either side of a curving country lane.
    Two long rows of dead landowners interlocking arms over the road
entangled in their own boundary fencing. A history of staking out territory
    of barbed wire as an agent of colony, holding in cattle/out people,
holding in people like cattle. It is a long strip of border dispute.
    From either end it is hard to unravel individuals with the eye.

When I was fifteen a spike of barbed wire punctured the front
    of my shin, a few inches above the ankle. It pierced my skin
pulled up as I pulled away, drawing a red line up. Blood
    or rust. I was in a group – walking – crossing a field hedge
in a place I did not know – an island between low and high lands.
    The leader wanted to cut my jeans to show the wound, the perfect
test of his first aid training. I wouldn't let him. I forget
    but my body remembers. Metal, rupture. The scar a bore hole,
a ritual circle with an avenue leading in or out of it, like a symbol
    for a secret element or astrological conjunction.

Dark hedges are oozing, weeping spikes of rust, twists of rust push
    through their skin like fences are meant to. Dark hedges
cry sticky dark tears, manifest sore red letters on their hivey skin
    – dermatographia – they are having a reaction and in their reaction
they are telling us the names of their aggressors, initial by initial,
    the dates of the attack – they are weeping, they are holding
each other where they can – while the jackdaws are screaming
    the small birds are screaming for the trees and the trees
keep growing, as they must, through restraint.

# Notes from a transect

## Breeding Bird Surveys

there are volunteers     there are square kilometres
twice a year they'll walk a transect
up the square and down and catch
every species that breeds there     there are gaps
in the data     the scientist says     it's hard
to ask questions     to prize apart     correlation
habitat or climate     disturbed or not
disturbed     perception or preconception
it depends what scale you concern yourself with

## People Against The Beaver

There are people against the beaver. They never
specify which beaver. I imagine one coppicing
willow illegally by the bank of a river
where watervoles swim in her wake, and a haze
of dragonflies veil her as she gnaws at the scrub
to build a damper outlaw nature.
How can they be against her? Her positive
story of translocation? Her fabulous
tail? That mysterious smile?

## Butterflies and Moths

we're on the cold edge     documenting decline
looking for correlation     with very
little control     we're on the cold edge
of where they live     working out
the why     the why     on the cold edge
is the next step we never get to

## What's Under Your Feet

Children dig for soil invertebrates, counting worms in the dirt.
A simple measure to track weather effects. Fingers
in the soil. Attending to what's beneath.

One school wins a visit from the scientist. When she asks
*does anyone have wildlife stories to share?*
the whole school put up their hands.


## Hunt Mentality

some folk will drive
hundreds of miles to see one offcomer bird

one rare visitor blown off course
one flapping signifier of global shifts

to tick a list/for the perfect shot
to keep it for their own/to own it


## Windows

Those lightless days when pain
keeps you in, under, and the feeder
at the window is the only source of movement

you count birds. A flurry of long-tailed tits
tumbling at the glass like blossom, the creep
of the nuthatch along the wall. There is no

zero count with a window survey.
Nothing so low, so empty, only
feathered need and flight.

## Restoration

*you can't go backwards in time*      as the scientist
said to the poet       conservation has to be
more than preventing change     we lose
a set of insects/a different set     comes in
     not necessarily better or worse
it might take a thousand years     or hundreds
to make something different    not better    not worse
what you need to understand is that change is real
is happening/has already happened    is not
natural    you can't go backwards in time


## Charismatic Animals

Is it cheaper to weep for a sea otter – clutching
paws in the water – than a lake? The scientist
herself is moved by ospreys. The poet
is guilty of magical thinking, reads
each tip of the barn owl's head as a message,
each heron as gift, each slow worm, each bee
as a personal envoy. Her neighbours. But the lake
is a grandmother. She has her own charisma.
She hides galaxies in her core with her gilly heart
as huge and as heavy as a moon.

# Bear in the Library

When you first hear it you are not sure
whether the bear is in your ear or the library.
Whether the bear is in your chest or the library.
When it growls again – the low, unthinking
growl of a bear lost in its reading –
you spot it. You try to stay calm. It is only
studying. It is only natural for a bear
to be growling a little as it turns the pages,
shuffling its haunches under the desk
in the library, on a snowy night.

In the café a woman asks "are you sure
it was a bear and not a tiger? Pouncey?"
You are sure. A bear is a bear, *inescapable*
*animal*, although the last wild bear
in this country was killed before the tenth century
like all great warriors, and it's been illegal
since 1835 to keep a bear
for baiting, to bait a bear, to keep
a bear for dancing since 1911.

*Everyone could use a bear sometimes*
but there's nothing worse than a bear in the library
*breathing at my side* when you're trying to write
and a poem sticks in your jaw, rewritten
for the bear ... *no one could say how the bear*
*got into the library* ... Poets are no longer
allowed to take bears into libraries, or lectures,
not since 1809, or enrol them
in university courses, whatever
their areas of interest. This bear is entirely
in charge of its programme of study. It is free,
or feral. Who am I to demand it not growl?

My love once lived on a road that was once
called Bear Ward Lane. I would visit him there,
where the bears and their keepers were kept, close
to the square where they fought and danced. The city

I had known became a place of bears,
of the persecution of bears, of poets
raised amongst bears, of people who lived
amongst bears, happy to hurt them. We gazed
at Bear Jars in the castle museum, their glossy
salt-glazed faces behind glass, muzzled,
learnt how they look like they're cuddling a cub,
but are wrestling a fighting dog. You pour
from the body of the bear; drink from its head.
They are chained together. This is local and particular.

In the library the lamps are lit. It is snowing
lightly but not sticking. You try to be pleased
that the bear is reading. *Good for you*, bear. Except
for the way it moves in the stacks, uncanny
on two legs, the way it turns the key
in the door with its paws after dinner, sure
it has every right to be there, browsing
the ancient copse of the shelves.

# Borders Gothic

You will meet it as a corner you cannot turn,
a gate flung open, a muffled struggle
offroad, in the woody murk where the old track
hums under mulch and brambles. You will be
a traveller in the midst, alone. It will throw itself
into your bag as a weight so heavy
you cannot go on. It will block your path
in the body of a bone white calf, or lady,
eyes like swollen moons, its voice
the splash of stones thrown in deep water.
It will howl. It will sit at your feet and sink
through the bog of the tarmac with a glug like a rock
or a woman being dropped in a mire. It will cry
three times from the shore. It will carry its coffin
or its head or its child in its hands. It will follow you
home. It will make you promises. You
will try to rid your house of it – the radiant
boy of it, heirloom drab of it – you will take it
still screaming, to sea, and drown it, you will bury it
day after day and find it always
back where it started, its lamp casting light
through every window, its small skull shrieking
*I know I know I know*

# Mountain

Scar on the skin of the land, hypertrophic, memory
of conflict, buckled and thickened by a difference
in process, grown out of accident, formed
out of pain. It says: this is where it hurt,
once, a long time ago. Earth
could have forgotten. Stone remembers.
Two worlds met here, connected, pressed
into one another, became something other.
Surrendered futures. They say:
this is where it hurt, when it happened,
and for a long time after. Sometimes
it still does. This is why we call them Fell.
Fateful, suspicious. Like all resurfacing
of selves we thought we had buried.

# Unwalking

We cannot set out not early no never – even late morning no
– not out – not in the mornings when our enemy gravity is the most
possible baggage and the world indecipherable the body its own
most possible baggage – property quite impossible to refuse – to simply
walk away from. This is not triviality.
It is violence to say to walk is human.

Refusal is our greatest blessing. Lightness is not a choice.

If I seem to you to be travelling light
it is because the infinite mass of my body
is non-apparent to the untrained observer.
The dead planet of me. By the time I am visible on earth
I will be nothing but dust and soundless echo.

To walk is not humane. Simply. It is not getting. Always, everywhere,
people have not walked, veining the earth with unpaths, unlines
of desire, so you have called them invisible. No footsteps. Others
– striked out – entirely ourselves – implying – to be consumed.

There are destinations without journeys, things you will never see if you
walk walk walk walk walk

Waiting is not the opposite of walking.
Unwalking is not the same as waiting.
I do not have to move to be moved. Are you moved?

The body is what I cannot untake with me what I cannot
leave behind what I cannot not discover, continually, along the way,
what I cannot undiscover, unhook myself from, slip my arms out from
like a rucksack, old baggage, old body, bag of rocks I carry with me.
My everything. What cannot be lost, on a walk an unwalk a wait or ever.

Two roads diverged in a yellow wood
And neither of them were accessible.
Two roads diverged in a wood and I –
I couldn't travel either of them.

The future is accessible: the most distant place
on an inaccessible road. With every step it seems to move further
and every step hurts. What is a sensible shoe to a sensible body?

I am all sensibility. I feel keenly. To walk is a risk and my relationship
to risk is fractious. I unwalk. I am very sensible.

Last time I was told to bring comfortable shoes
I replied 'there are no comfortable shoes
unless you can bring me a comfortable body.'
No one offered me a comfortable body.

This is what I learnt in the course of unwalking.
When I spend a day I feel exhausted – so I pace – a quality
of attention which is an excellent thing.

Every dislocation is equally important or unimportant, the joints
turning wrong, doubling back in the most lonely places.

Unlovely, undemocratic, unreasonable.
The line of unwalking is persistent self-interest.

We must become experts if the body is to articulate itself, not
dearticulate itself. This is not so much unromantic as reasonable.
Knees, hips, ankles, wrists are natural halting places.
Walking is not so much romantic as unreasonable, the flavour
of walking too rare and too extraordinary.

Any walk an expedition when to unwalk is quite ordinary, unexceptional,
just what we do, daily, unwalking in all weathers every season of the body,
unwalking a continuum upon which the least emphatic
occurrences are registered clearly.

Any stickman, through long use, will adjust itself to the pain.
(If you're fit to walk they'll declare you fit for work)

There are so many ways through a landscape we cannot choose.
The project of an unwalk will be to remain adequate.
One continues through effort of will not fidelity – there is no fidelity –
there is no natural span. This is what we have survived.

We who unwalk are not without value.
We are not without value. We are not without.

This is the largest experience we can have.

There are walks on which I lose myself, become two places.
There are walks on which I lose.

The horizon grows wider, the hills gather round.
They will not return me, to myself, or at all.

# queen of the woods

the green queen of the woods is dead     I found her
skull becoming the forest floor     transmuting to moss
waving towards the thin light as fronds    so damp
with reaching    whilst also    sinking    becoming
earth    whilst also    rising out of it
a magnificent mushroom    greening from grey
with eye sockets and nasal sockets and the stubs
of horns    like the god she is    scattering
herself out into it    the green    re
becoming    feral    lost    the queen
of the woods is dead    long live the queen
of the woods    long may she thrive may she thrive

## *Motacilla flava flavissima*

When you came to us in the grey yard
it was out of the darkest season
the first bright day
               brightest of bright
challenging to identify at the time
                              the trees
black streaks with sticky buds like rain drops
against the grey-green fell
                    you flew
out of the lightless mouth of winter
with the sun in you
               most yellow of yellows
the sun in you
                the sun trailing after
the spinning rock of your body
                    blazing yellow
spreading yellow with every dab of your tail
the train of a comet
                the augur you were
you must have flown into the darkness and found
the sun by the thin arc of yellow escaping
from the well where she had been buried
                              I thought
you must have carried the sun in your beak
like a seed
          that you jolted and swallowed her yellowest
of all yellows
          most yellow
                    most bright
                         you coughed her
out from your perch on the splintering fence
and filled your mouth with nest stuff instead
you stayed with us
                chose us
                    you built your yellow
world in the cracks in our grey one lit up
with yellow
          yellow glowed from the fissures
in the slate

31

they call you a migrant breeder
when you turn to red a passage visitor
you knit your home in the passage between houses
the passage between one and another
                              your yellow
between
          your yellow
                    lighting the way

II

# Dorothy's Rain

rains     frosty     moonlight     heavy
rain     amber     clouds     lighter
rain     showers     lightning     & showery
rain     little rain     rainy     misty
rain     heavy rain     rain     all day
Very rainy—all day     Rain!     Rain!
Rain comes on     Rainy morning
wet evening     showers     a little Rain     Misty
rain     Rain     all day     Rain
comes on     hail     & rain all day.     Lightning
heavy     rain comes on.     Showers &c
&c Rain     sleet &c—     &c Storm
rain     rain     comes on in the evening
rain all night     rainy morning
rain in showers     writing/resting
very rainy all day     Rain comes on
In frost     rain     & mist – clears
No rain     A little Soft Rain     Rain
All day     rain     Very rainy     cold
Very rainy     very dark     Dark & lovely
no rain     Rain showers     After rains 2 larks
His love     Enchanting frosty rain
Rain     rain     Rainy     rainy
& flood     drizzling rain     very wet     rain
breaks     more rain     rain     raining
rain     small soft rain     but raining
cold & rainy     a little gloom at night
a few drops of rain     starlight     rain
a little rain     a little     rain     a little
rain     mist     rain     no downright
rain     but much refreshing downfall
never all-day rain     & often delightful
rain     rainy     with rain     rain
not heavy     rain     Thunder in air
very close & fast     Thunder showers     head-ache
Very wet & close     Heavy rains     rain
no rain     rainy     no storms after all
a veil of mist     mild rain     rain
at night     rainy     rainy     a woman

killed by lightning      rain in night
clashing sounds      very rainy      now
again hearing rain      rain comes on heavy
as soon as I reached home      coldish
and rain comes on      heavy rain      heavy shower
heavy rain in evening      sheet lightning      & distant
thunder      very gloomy & threatening      rain
showery      rain in the night      slight rain
gloomy gloomy gloomy      but pleasant
through showers      showery      very showery      rather
heavy      rain      throwing off her damp coverings
I never saw her so thin      Showers      a few slight
showers      wet morning      wet afternoon      wet evening
rainy night      and excessive clearness of the air
before bed time, a heavy      rain      rainy
rain      rain      came on during
rain      comes on before      very rainy
a shower comes on      & rain      continues
by a note      all the way stormy      showery
very wet in evening      rain      showers
driven back by rain      heavy      rain
at night      very rainy      heavy rain
& heavy in the night      heavy rain      rainy
rainy streaming rain when they left us      caught
in rain      heavy rain      rain again      rainy
mizzly rain      heavy rain      some rain      but improving
rain      heavy rain      our eyes      all un
expectedly open on a rainy morning
rainy      slight rain      heavy rain      slight
rain      showery at noon & rainy
afternoon rain      very rainy      rainy morning
rainy evening      showers but not heavy      showers
as light as possible      with showers      showery
day with fine gleams as usual      showery
heavy      rain      one slightest of showers
rain comes on      heavy rain comes on
rain at night      heavy rain      heavy rain
rainy      drizzly rain      very rainy      a shower
comes on      showery      showery with a gleam
or two      all day      rain      impossible
glorious silver drops      smoky

steam    yellow lights    rainbow complete
rainy    rainy    with intermissions
rainy    showery with gleams    storm
& rain    stormy & gleamy    all day
showers    showery    rain comes on
blustering with gleams    very stormy & wet
rain    so heavy    fierce storm    heavy showers
still showery    storm & rain pouring    rain
heavy rain at night    rainy    drizzling
rain in night heavy    rain at night rainy
slight rain    mizzy    rain    heavy
rain    rainy    but not so bad
without rain    rainy    rain comes on
heavy rain    rainy    not throughout rainy
heavy rain    rain    more or less    though not heavy
rain    rain    very stormy and evil
rain    with tempestuous gushes    a letter
with good reports of weather    Flood in night    teaming
ceaseless − such Rushes +    Torrents of Rain
a struggle towards moonshine    with much rain    heavy
rain comes on    rain    heavy before comes
on very very    rainy fields flooded
in the night    slight rain    rainy    very stormy
rain    very rainy    comes on quite a storm
a few drops of rain    slight rain    rains most
but no rain    a few drops    of rain    a good deal
of rain    rain    in gloom & rain
fog    & rain    with warmth    rainy
rainy    rainy    slight rain    rain
rain    without rain    rain but not heavy
walked towards rain    rain    heavy rain
heavy rain    rain stops us    slight rain    rainy
rain    very rainy    rain    rain & twilight
rain    rainy    rainy    rainy
heavy rain    heavy rain    rain falling without respite
rain    rainy rain    comes on    rain
but rain    rainy    heavy rain    threatening
rain    rather gloomy    thundering rain    heavy
rain    comes on till evening    in rain
rain    slight rain    gentle rain    gentle rain
threatening rain    Rain!    Rain.

## Much With Body

Very beautifully & glad
rain will come
but only a small shower
        convalescent
in spite of Rain.
        I was fatigued
& weak & though
in little pain
        could not see past
not a drop of rain
        & Rain before night
           & from the day
to the present    clear
with a few large shapes of busy    clouds
 & us    dullish & turbulent
& the rains    moderate. I begin to read
the Life    the sum    of my reading. Fair
or nearly so

(I was tired
        & only)

★

The night very stormy. Very ill. Why
or wherefore I know not − pain − sickness −
head-ache − perspiration − heat & Cold −
exhausted & free from pain, I slept

& a hail shower falls from dazzling silver
& dark clouds to remind us not to expect
a calm. This evening, very stormy, rain
by pailfuls driven against my windows.

★

After a stormy
          night clouds
dazzling white
          & dark & snow
& now & then
          a glittery hailshower
& a moon
          & all things glittery


                              ★


Cold sun by bright big clouds grows calmer.
Sat some hours with the rain, stormy rain.

I am wonderfully Re-established. & stormy.
A conclusive article against reform.

Cast out the same parts of our venerable bright moon.
I am not able to hear prayers.


                              ★


Large dazzling clouds visit me. Amiable,
blustering. Letters from a lost dismal house.
In night, tremendous showers streaming down
my windows.              Tolerable, but very dark.
Much harmed by sudden warnings, we are
again fixed in my still helpless state
in convulsions – & much with body.


                              ★

Fearful rain.
       Pailfuls of rain
in the night & fierce lashes.
              Tremendous wind
& rain in a quiet
         moment & storm
come back
     as bad as ever.


★


Blustering better. No fits. Doing well
& unexpectedly raining by fits.

Trials smoothly over and of no importance.
And showers & almost unable to speak.

Letters smoke below stairs.


★


The rain will not depart from its accustomed strongholds.
A glittering shower travels over us.

I have been sticking leafy green twigs of Elder
among my Spring and Winter flowers

my garden all of the seasons visited
by bees, taking no rest.


★


Misty muzzling bird chaunting morning
gone off in this misty rain. I was very

poorly last night – from pain & – better –
still in pain. I am weakly therefore

afraid to go down. Afraid of the fatigue
of down stairs. Better, though in pain. Butterflies

and bees amid my gardens. I am free
from pain & I could not join in prayers.

★

Very bright frosty air – very tempting –
but no!
        Not strong enough in limbs
to be willing
            to rise – lay down. Bright day
but dangerous
      – alas! Poor prisoners!
                      A fine
bright morning. Slept Sweetly. Very
sick    & a deep sleep
follows the cold fine moon.

★

My flowers everlasting. I long to be out.
How I long to be free in the open air, birds
all singing, the earth & air preparation
for worship & rest from slaughter. Something
in the air oppresses. I am not well.

Still they tell me the air is too cold for me.
To go out & feel it – the blighting wind
bars me up. Helpless household.
My little cell, glorious red
of anenomes. My treasure all winter.

41

I suffered much (sickness & pain)     and continue it
I durst not go out and I much stronger I shall not
get out I was ill I cannot go out weak and languid I rose
driven to bed by sickness bile thrown up rose as usual
forced back to bed & very unwell yet not much pain very
poorly not not in great pain I lay     chill
dark & wholly unable to read unfit to talk     unable


★


Rain continues. Green things burst
marvellously into light. Thunder
calls but I cannot see her. Strength
much beaten. This should have been May day. Trees
bursting but I am imprisoned. Sickness,
much rain. I am lazy and have no pleasure.
Tolerably free from pain attacks.
I am no company. Showers sting me.
I mend, slowly. Pining
earth – transplanted – restored.


★


Rain and the dismal labour of walls
          fills the rooms with the road, advances
with speed small red roses & green
          small leaf. But that is beautiful, solitary
at my request. A sweet gleamy morning
          supplied me with various flowers till my legs
bear me up no longer, traveller.
          Poor thing! She has a weaning expectation.
I do not venture out.


★

The air very soft and sacred and one
long fit of pain. Often very well
for an invalidish body. Could hardly speak
most strangely & the cold edging off. A brilliancy
surpassing anything I saw at that hour.
The air does me good. I feel it restored
to light. I have taken a walk in the house.
Something oppresses me. The wildness of nature
with elaborate formality. At night not well
for I was oppressed & very uneasy.
To see me in the fresh air on grass.

★

I rose – disappointed – tired & in pain.
There is a forlorn almost branch when I lie
on my bed, I would not part with.

Death – or perhaps I mistake – in excellent
health & spirits – at my door – but I could not
see her. I was very poorly all evening

& could not
have journeyed
up stairs.

★

I have had much pain.
Dark winds blowing – showers gathering.

Heavy rain. So ill
as not to be able to dress. My limbs

like marble. Again in much pain. Rain
rain & gently but rain

★

With stillness I keep pretty comfortable.
Flash of lightning, with thunder close

– & at night also the showers very heavy –
caught in Great Showers I am very comfortable

but in evenings pain & my limbs grow stronger
and the swelling is less    with invisible rain.

# Mortification/Frequent Shipwrecks

This rain must make & keep
all persons & things dull. A great
mortification; frequent shipwrecks.

I do not regain my strength.
I do not get as well as before.

Blustering weather and self, weakly.
I feel the cold sadly, sadly after
a dreadful stormy rainy night.

The cold air wrecks me.
I am fearful of the air

this cold! this cold alas! alas!
disordered within uneasy & weakly
feeble with exertion.

So long have I been idle,
oppressive with dullness & dark. Nothing
remarkable. I do not gather strength.

Very dark melancholy myself.
Whistling wind and blue. Weakness
oppresses me. Dismal doom. Torments.

Night is here to tell me.

III

# Epiphany Insomnia

When I close my eyelids I'm not shutting out light, I'm drawing the blinds.
The light source is internal. It's like draping a cloth over a tv
when the tv is still on, sound blaring, mouthing drama.
Behind my eyelids the light is blue and cold like screen light, agitating,
the projections thrown on their walls and the animating source.
I lay down my head on the pillow ready to vanish, unconscious,
and the carousel starts up, incandescence and music, grinning horses.

We all know this one. Inappropriate flippancy of the wakeful body,
the blanket and the chair, the hot water bottle
like a life-raft in the frozen sea of the night, the cat
unsettled by our catlike watchfulness. How our body disturbs,
swimming round the night house, alarmed by gravity.
Sleeplessness is contagious. We are quarantined
somewhere between a vision state and an open-edged dream.

# Breath Test

My breath got lost in the post. I sent
a box of it out, portioned in six
foil bags like space food rations. I addressed it
as instructed, sent it away, a long
exhale. Bated breath. It arrived

back at my door in the arms of the postman –
a large brown box of my breath – marked
*addressee gone away.* I held my breath
to my chest. My breath weighed next to nothing.

I had wasted my breath. It was a time
of crisis. I had to post my breath
to the hospital, to keep the hospital secure.
I could not go to the hospital and breathe.

I caught my breath. Six silver bags
like emergency blankets around my breath
mirrors to breathe on to check if you're living.
I took my breath away. My breath

returned to sender. It was not a love letter.
It was not a request. It was innovation.
I could not breathe at the hospital. It was
a time of crisis. It was a test.

I wanted to save my breath, but my breath
was out of me. I could not draw breath in
only let it go again, hoping
it held itself long enough to arrive
like a kiss on the wind, still fresh.

# Gravitas/Rumination Subscale

Every point mass attracts every single
other point mass by a force acting
along the line intersecting – can I keep
on falling interminably? – the force is proportional
to the product of the masses and inversely proportioned
to the square of the distance between them. The sound
that falls from my mouth like a plumb line when my knee
hits the ground. The crack of a thin bone placed
under pressure from the right direction or slap
of palm on ice. This is the law.
I anxiously want. I anxiously want.
I am a point mass falling, blood
sloshing down the slouching stocking of a body
any time I let it act on me, inciting it
by standing, invoking it any time I rise.
I cannot seem to keep it out of my mind. Are we
going to rise up? And fall down again, sickened
and dizzy with the dream of rebellion, counter
the tyranny of downward motion. Of the planet's
dense core. I keep thinking about how badly I want.
This is the relationship between the motion of the moon
and the motion of a body falling. If the bodies
in question have spatial extent. If the bodies
are in question. If the bodies have attraction as all
massive bodies must do, for each other, for the sky
and the centre. It is unavoidable. I keep thinking
how badly I want the pain to stop.
I anxiously. I catastrophically. I
massively. I subject to scalar gravity. I
stand and let go. I kiss the earth.
This is serious.
I keep thinking about how much it hurts.

# Paper Pellets on a Saucer

I have been discreetly making allowances for everyone else's derangement
which is intolerable. When I look at water in sun I think
*they winked their ice-hard dynamics* I hear

*tappity*
                    *tap tappity tap*

what I wanted was *a thinking-place of green corridors*

but there are diamonds in the wholemeal, in the plaster saints, smashed up,
in the herring roe, in the wheelchair, in the red herring of healing, disability,
in *moist pale layers of embryo fish*

sometimes I cannot tell the difference between the real and illusory

*embroiled in a psychic allegory* in which I am an author, or a grandmother
plotting in a cottage, warming my dissociation by a two-barred heater, doing
*everything very slowly but with extreme attention*

as though to avoid a drowning or a subplot involving diabolism

there are the dusty back shelves of a bookshop, figs in syrup, a sinister
friend, the irregular *tap click tap* turning up phrases like *paper pellets*
*on a saucer*        unrepeatable        unrecordable        in chorus

*the way you notice absurd details, it's absurd of you*

I too am *too ignorant to be a witch.*
I am *off like someone taking a plunge against nature.*
When I sleep I disappear as a matter of course

*we are all a little mad in one or other particular*

someone asks about my book and I think *do they mean*
*the book [I'm] writing or the one in which [I] live?*
If anyone is listening, let them take note.

*Of course they are symbols, but they are also voices.*

52

The Typing Ghost has not recorded any lively details about this poem.
The reason is The Typing Ghost doesn't know how to describe this poem.
*I have an independent life.*

*Pain convinces me that I'm not wholly a fiction.*

If you have no private life whatsoever
there is no knowing where you go in your privacy. You might
step into your room and simply disappear.

# Unknowing

I have believed in you, in the sharpness of understanding.
I have felt you ticking in the lea of my ribs,
wheezing outrageously into my chest.
Cognition living in a deadly firmament.
I have believed in my special beholding.
Your mysterious aetiology, your crooked intent.

I have woken in the night, you the spoke
pinning me to pain or the wanting of bodily
light. The clean and ghostly thing
pressing against my will or witting.
*Privy spirit, whose dooms be hid.*
I have thought upon the naked being of you.

I have unworshipped you. I have sat
in square brown chairs in consulting rooms
stared down by truths, and agreed to forget you.
*Incomprehensible to created knowledgeable powers.*
How many men, old with doubt,
touched where you touched me; claimed to feel nothing?

You are the stirring of clear discerning
that presses upon me, will bear me down.

I dared not speak with my blabbering tongue
of these quaint heats, a grumbling fastened
in my fleshly heart, owned and congealed
with the substance of my being. Ghostly spouse.
Darkly painted. No other thing
but myself. The foul stinking lump of myself.

I feel the preciousness of your growth with a listy
love. I comprehend you now.
Your wisdom is your deepness. Illumined by grace.
Manifest sorrow. This little pressing
of being, this cumbrous mass of unknown.
Forgive me, I have been led into much error.

I have worked against the course of nature.
You are the substance of all good living
and without you no good work may be done.
You are full ready, and abideth me.
I am your shell. You are my becoming.
I desire this not to unbe.

# The Long Dance

*Dear God, poor Du Fu, I thought: It's the poetry again.* – Don Paterson

This is how it starts. The shoes dance towards you,
about you, skittish as the deer you meet
at twilight at the brink of the woods, who seem
to be waiting for you to follow the path
they've beaten through the scrub, the way they pause,
turn to you, watch till you move to move on,
and so you follow, glowing with stealth
like the moon, and if the moon is huge
as a pool-light in the night-window of the lake, you can't
be blamed if your body tips to its gravity,
tumbles into its luminous mouth
and through it. This is how it gets you

you write because you have to. You write until it hurts
in the bones and tendons of your hand, under
the covers after lights out, under the desk
when you should be attending to other lessons,
your fingers ink-stained and bent to requirements
of the pen. Long after you switch to computer
from paper your hand retains the callous
cushion of the pen-rest on your middle digit,
how it pushed the distal phalange away
from the rest of you, marking its own direction.
You think this sign will always be with you
but one year it's gone. No warning. The body

resets, recovers, finds its route
like water, the law of least resistance.
You write to live. You try to live well.
To keep moving. To watch from the treeline. To make
the fall a long dance. To come back down
from the trees to your fireside, your solid stone walls,
week after week, year after year.
To remember the moon is a portal. To not reach
when you don't want to travel. The shoes inch toward you,
nuzzle your ankles. Warm breath, soft tongues.
Of course, you put them on.
You let them put you on.

v/s

## Monthlies

My monthlies are not
your monthlies. My monthlies
come dressed up as a 16 gauge needle
swinging an empty pint-sized tote
and a bag of saline. I am no good
with emptiness. My body wants volume.
Take take take. My monthlies insist
they are saving my life, on my body's failure
to give enough up, on my body's peculiar
habit of hoarding hot metal like stolen
trophies, stashing iron in the back
corners of all of my organs as though
I am living alone in a mansion and have to
fill every room with scrap as though
it's a pathological love of things
that brings me back to this ward, this green
vinyl bed by the french door, this plastic
pillowcase, month on month.

# Slitting the vein

If it sounds gynaecological *vene/*
*section* everyone knows the letter
v and a woman the letter v and
blood the letter v is vaginal. I've
seen *The Vagina Monologues.* I know
just shouting V is vaginal. V! I
think of mediaeval wound men, the slit
in the side of Christ, disciples sticking
their hands in, how it is drawn as a cervix,
the slip from womb to wound, of how
I need to be bled because I don't bleed
enough because I need to be bled,
that women are expected to bleed, of
the locum who shrugged *women bleed*
when all my blood was falling out
at once in shiny clots like pastilles –
I'm always either too much or not
enough – they open my veins like
portals. It sounds more bloody
than it needs to. I have to
explain over and over
the word the meaning
the thing in itself
why we call it v/s
but I'm a quick study
naturalised the needle
like a quill in the elbow
in no time really –
the abbrev.
the sharp
the cu( )t.

## Leeches

Leeches have three hundred teeth. Leeches
leave a bite mark like a peace sign. Leeches excrete
anaesthetic when they pierce your skin,
like Emla cream. Leeches are precious.
A medicinal leech is hard to find.

We are listening to the radio on the drive to the hospital.
*Natural Histories*. A half hour of leeches.
A leech is doctor. A leech is a fiend
who sucks you dry. A leech is a bad
friend. A good leech will save lives.

Leeches are curious. Leeches migrate
around a body. Victorians tied
strings to their leeches and let them roam,
mine the body's unseen continents,
drain what they couldn't control. I consider

the grace of leeches. The diaspora of leeches.
The harvesting of leeches to extinction. An old man
reads a young man's poem, in which
a leechgatherer on a lonely moor becomes
a beautiful cure: the last leech in England

and I think of him now – as I lay on my bed,
a needle in each elbow crook, the cold
saline dripping in, the hot
blood dripping out – skulking in a pool
on the weary moor, a small striped ghost

very beautiful, very precious, very good.

# Mast Year/Helplessness Subscale

beech shells falling a storm of them sheeting
down siling down it is terrible
and I think it is never going to get any better
plut plut plut plut on the cobbles huge
rippling drops falling to a swelling
flood sinking into the mud then welling
out of the mud it is awful and I feel
that it overwhelms me the ground throwing
them up as the branches throw them down
the lane drowned under the sudden river
washed clean of itself I worry all the time
about whether the pain will end and they
become the lane and the lane crunches
under your feet I feel I cannot
stand it any more with each
step into winter I feel I cannot
go on which might last seven years
which you may emerge from altered owing
some kind of tithe there is nothing I can do
to reduce the intensity of the pain

# Sick Girl Theory

The first time we talked properly      when you made a point
of talking to me      you had suspicions
the dim pub full of amateur inventors      you took me aside
told me about us      how same we were
our flimsy hearts      tedious resilience
how much shared      drew on the back
of my hand the makeup you'd bought that day –
an eyeliner that changed colour when you smoothed a gloss over

you didn't know it was long past changing.
Done for months. I knew what you were doing
making yourself real to me      as though that could help anything.

I couldn't sleep that night      had betrayed both of us
given up both of us surrendered us both

all night still with the curve of eyeliner & shimmer
of green–gold you marked on my hand

I vibrated with belatedness. There were too many of me/
you. Replaceable.      In the darkest hour
thought about removing the one of us I had access to

thought of our bodies and what made us good substitutes.
Sick girls. Weak girls.      How the orange light leaching
through the blinds at 5am was code alerting me, finally,
that that was how he chose us, because he knew how to get us
to let him in      tired girls      confused in our dream states, chronic
with persuadability      he knew where to punch
to keep our hearts beating. And where to stop them.
He knew where our skin was too thin.

# Teething/Magnification Subscale

In the twelfth month of the year of the plague
a piece of my tooth falls off. I wonder
whether something serious may happen. I swallow it
before I know it. In all my dreams of teeth falling
they fall outwards, not inwards. They tumble from my mouth
like hailstones from a cloud. I become afraid
that the pain will get worse. Within me, the sliver
of my broken tooth roots, grows limbs, spawns.
Indestructible. Inevitable. All my dreams
come true but I cannot read them. I keep thinking
of other painful events. My tongue
troubles the stump with its branches shorn off.
It reminds me of something I've not understood,
of something to come. The Dentist says
it's a clean break, I'm lucky, the tooth is healthy.
He polishes the cutting edge smooth.

# Your ex-first-love is an internet guru, and this is what he says

Inside your heart is a little child, longing to be set free. It is imprisoned
by all the 'shoulds' you impose upon it. It is no coincidence
that the words 'heart' and 'hurt' are so similar. Things grow
& change more in warmth. We keep food cold to stop it changing.
Keep your heart cold & life will never change.
How many words do we need to point us back to our heart?

If you are prone to fear then your heart needs strengthening.
The best way is vigorous exercise, like running, cycling, hill walking etc.
Your heart is literally a portal, a doorway for your consciousness
so you can move from a shadowy realm into a totally luminous one.
Trying to solve problems with a problematic mind is like trying to clean
dirty dishes with a dirty sponge. You must first clean the sponge.

The most effective way to respond to fearful thoughts is to bring
attention out of your mind, into your body. Then relax your body.
To choose harmony, just stop thinking. Do you ever get lost
in thoughts? especially all the thoughts that make us feel weak.
You cannot know who you are through thinking. Beautiful friends
I hope this speaks to your heart in a powerful way.

Healthier choices lead you to feeling stronger. Unhealthy choices
lead you to feeling weaker. Are you regularly giving your attention
to trivialities, distractions, superficial entertainment etc?
Our mind is often occupied with thoughts. The addiction
to mentally knowing has to be completely let go of.
Just find something to care about, big or small.

Focus your mind on one intention, and fill your heart
with one desire: to alleviate suffering in this world.

Then begin with yourself. The good news is that no effort
is required. I assure you that the Universe is fully aware of you
and desires loving Reunion. We are all children.
Everything will make sense when you clear your mind
of all thought-based interference, and you become a clear channel
for universal energy. This entire Universe is 100% on your side.

Tune in to the G R AT I T U D E channel.
Forget everything you've ever read, heard, seen or thought.

Make sure you sit down and observe your thinking mind.
It is dysfunctional and many are afraid of it. Make friends with it.
You are not a bad person. You do not want other people to suffer.
So there is no need to feel guilty about enjoying life the way you want.

If we stop caring, we experience more darkness in our lives;
but fortunately the remedy is obvious. We just start caring.
This is enough. Our heart wants to be deeply excited.
There is no need to feel lost or abandoned or doomed.

We are not perfect, but we do have a heart that cares. Sometimes
it cares so much that we feel the need to control things.

We wish to punish the bad, but they are ill. The ego
gets obsessed with its own progression, even spiritually. Tomorrow
you have another opportunity to be kind to all the people you meet.
Around 7 billion people need your help. What can you do?

The mind is hungry to know because it has become addicted to thought.
Be a clear channel, free of mental distortion. You cannot mentally
understand it all. Imagine if a fish could communicate with the water.
Could you prove conclusively to a blind man that there is a golden disc
of fire moving slowly across the sky? I hope you enjoy this special video.
I hope this simple little video speaks to your heart.

The men walking the streets with machine-guns, they have a heart.
They are doing their job, and they have heart.
They are not there to hurt people,
and I do not believe they want to hurt people.

Feel free to follow me.
                              Feel free to follow me.
After reading this book, it will be impossible
to unconsciously create suffering for yourself ever again.

# Sword dance in the museum garden

Sword as mirror
                    sky flash
                            portal
of light
          rain dropping from the broken
                                  gutter

bird cut
          drip
               blue sky scissor

meniscus of movement
                    silver
                        the long

sweep of your arm
                  warrior
                      cloud circle

waxing
          in the hands
                  the sword
                          is a sickle

I am
      harvesting
                clouds
                      clouds of [chi].

# Girl Poets

The girl poets are unconvincingly heightened.
They are ground-breaking and important. It is a shame.
They live in unassuming vignettes
fuzzy with new possibilities          intellectually
abstruse.          The girl poets could be in trouble.
The girl poets are not an idle concern.

Their poems were born in the rubbish tip          awkward
and misunderstood. Their poems are creatures
we can never approach          boxes of trinkets
          decorative and over-designed          crude
with sentimentality          like internet censorship.
Their best poems are double          faced.

The girl poets are lexicographical conjecture.
They are trivial          beasts          stalking themselves
down streets of dissenting cities          tailing
versified intelligence at the supermarket          aimed
and aimless          drawn by the superficial tingle
of their mildly irritating electric heat.

The girl poets are successful and very presentable.
Slight          brusque          tricky. They pummel
with chatty allusion          childlike. They bark.
They cannot be taken seriously          wearing
as they will          warm and woolly          restless
feelings          (like the best and worst of this style).

The girl poets live like they write          with charming
clumsiness          unconvincing          florid
with earnestness. It blooms          sixth-formy          from
their oblique and gracefully elaborate skin.
The girl poets are working harder          transformed
into soaring birds.          The girl poets win.

# An Aubade upon St Lucy's Day

*I am every dead thing in whom Love wrought new alchemy.* – John Donne

It is Friday the 13th – the morning of the year's
midnight – the weak sun rising from a vast
bank of cloud like a late dawn – unavoidable
delay – and the snow flaring on the tops,
the first bright thing in days. But it's just
a squib. *The world's whole sap is sunk.*
And you are waking up again in November
2016 in your studio flat
in the Southside, cracking your limbs out, breath
rolling snowballs in the halflight. You know the news
before checking the stolen internet. You feel it
in the frozen cores of your bones, in the clutching
of your stomach in the cold. The gas fire won't spark.
You've fed all your coins to the snarky mouth
of the electricity meter but something is wrong
with the wiring and the light keeps failing. You turn

and wake into June, dawn chorus drowned out
by a storm. When you open your curtain you find
a dead bee on the sill. Yesterday at the polling
station you saw the carpark scattered
with shattered glass where a car accelerated
from the exit sign into a wall

and it is 1791 and it is very heaven
because you can't hear the whoosh/clonk of the guillotine –
you are young – it is out of your range – or see
the blood or heads pooling in the squares, or the barricades
falling. Bliss in that dawn to be alive!

but it is 1793 and in the square the women are knitting
and it is 2011 and in the square the tanks are coming
and it is 1989 and in the square the tanks are coming
and the soldiers are coming the soldiers are always coming

it is unscientific of course to call
today the year's midnight, it's dark enough
but the longest dark is to come. Luminous
anachronism, to dream it stops here, like arranging
your eyes on a plate and expecting a vision.
We're revolving towards it, the long night's festival

and it is 2010 and you are thinking it can never
get worse than this, and it is 2015
and worse, and 2017 and worse,
this is it, you are sure this is it, it is worst,

you would recognise the worst when you sank in it, but shadows
keep growing, like this morning which is every time
you have sunk back certain you are in it, the deep
dark of things which are not, but are not

while the world keeps drowning. Everyone thinks
they are voting to protect what they love, like everyone
thinks they are good. We can't all be good.
Some of us have to lose/be lost.
Some of us have to be loved, and forsaken.

There is a dead bee curled behind a curtain
and a car on its roof by an exit sign, spinning
slower than a planet on an arbitrary axis
and we are all going nowhere in it, we are upside
down, trapped, waiting for someone
to come and put us right, to pull
us out but no one is coming because
we told them we wanted full control
when we agreed to discontinue the sun.

# When All This Is Over Is Over

When all this is over I mean[1]
to travel north, by the high[2]
unapproved roads[3]

through silver birch and pine[4]
each body a lion of courage[5]
feeding redwoods[6]

stalking the shoreline,[7]
probably in June[8]
when all this is over.[9]

When all this is over we'll follow a path.[10]
When all this is over I plan[11]
to go north.[12]

There will be no god when this is over.[13]
Rolling their trash bins out,
after all of this is over.[14]

When all this is over, I mean to retire, where[15]
I have made of my life something particular, and real[16]
from the mossy mountainsides.[17]

Here is what I will miss.[18]
When it's over, I want to say.[19]
Nobody will have heard about my special skills[20]

when all this is over, I mean.[21]

1 Kathleen Jamie, 'Lochan'
2 Kathleen Jamie, 'Lochan'
3 Siobhan Campbell, 'When all this is over'
4 Jane Clarke 'When all this is over'
5 Mary Oliver 'When Death Comes'
6 Jenny Qi 'When all this is over'
7 Jenny Qi 'When all this is over'
8 Kathleen Jamie, 'Lochan'
9 Eiléan Ní Chuilleanáin 'Swineherd'
10 Jane Clarke 'When all this is over'
11 Siobhan Campbell, 'When all this is over'
12 Jane Clarke 'When all this is over'
13 Ruth Awad 'The One where I beg'
14 Ada Limón, 'Dead Stars'
15 Eiléan Ní Chuilleanáin 'Swineherd'
16 Mary Oliver 'When Death Comes'
17 Jane Clarke 'When all this is over'
18 Jenny Qi 'When all this is over'
19 Mary Oliver 'When Death Comes'
20 Eiléan Ní Chuilleanáin 'Swineherd'
21 Kathleen Jamie, 'Lochan'

# Sky with Northern Bottlenose Whales

This morning I lay in bed and watched the clouds move
swimming toward the blue shining
open mouth of the loch        sky whales
beasties the length of a village        entirely
at home        they belong        anywhere        breathing
flotilla        you can see their hearts pulse through
their heavy bellies        see how their under
carriage is darker        this is specific
to their species        see how they keep together
this is how they choose to live        never
lonely in wandering        herding slowly
away to the deeper horizon where they can
expand        dive        feed on what
they desire        on what they need

# Sailing by Silvership

The moon is a ship
and we are sailing in her

how can we not talk about her?

She glistens
and we glisten

she throws out nets of herself, trailing

clouds like weeds
and we walk them as bridges

to the stars, arm in arm, singing.

And the stars themselves
are glistening      aren't they?

like specks of quartz in dark rock, spangling

the great unknowable
expanse as it squeezes

into this particular wedge of night

the swell of this road
the dark fell sea

soon, we will be there, sister

waving from the deck
of the one you call

dipper — *so big we can sit in it!* — no

so big
it will carry us away.

# Notes & Acknowledgements

Many thanks to all who supported my work during the writing of this collection, including Gladstone's Library, for a residency in 2018; Arts Council England, for a DYCP grant in 2019; Cove Park, for a residency in 2020; and New Writing North, for granting the work in progress a Northern Writer's Award, 2020.

'Fell' is included in *Women On Nature* ed. by Katharine Norbury (Unbound, 2021). An early version of 'Isolation Blessing' was published online on *Write Where We Are Now* (MMU, 2020). 'Frog Season' and 'Pond life' are published in *The Scores*, 6. 'Habitats' was placed third in the Rialto Nature and Place Poetry Competition, 2017. 'Notes from a transect' was commissioned for *Magma 71: The Climate Change Issue*. 'Bear in the Library' quotes or misquotes lines from Vahni Capildeo, Emma Jones and Chrissy Williams. 'Borders Gothic' is published in *The Lonely Crowd*, (August 2019). 'Unwalking' was written as part of a collaboration with Harry Josephine Giles and Vahni Capildeo in response to Thomas A. Clark's 'In Praise of Walking'. '*Motacilla flava flavissima*' is published in *Watch the Birdie* (Beautiful Dragons Press, 2018).

All the text in 'Dorothy's Rain', 'Much With Body' and 'Mortification/ Frequent Shipwrecks' is found from transcriptions made by Dr Emily Stanback and Dr Anastasia Stelse of Dorothy Wordsworth's late journals, held in manuscript at The Wordsworth Trust, Grasmere.
'Dorothy's Rain' is found from:
        DCMS 104.1 December 1 1824 – December 9 1825
        DCMS 104.3 June 29 – September 24 1826
        DCMS 118.1 January 21 – August 9 1830
        DCMS 118.2 Aug 9 1830 – February 12 1831
        DCMS 118.3 Feb 12 1831 – September 7 1833
'Much With Body' is found from DCMS 118.4 February 6 – October 3 1834. 'Mortification/Frequent Shipwrecks' is found from DCMS 118.5 October 4 1834 – November 4 1835.

'Monthlies' and 'Leeches' are published in *Gush* (Frontenac House, 2018). 'Slitting the vein' appeared on 'And Other Poems'. 'Gravitas/Rumination Subscale', 'Mast Year/Helplessness Subscale', and 'Teething/Magnification Subscale' use language from The Pain Catastrophizing Scale, commonly used in Cognitive Behaviour Therapy and other psychological pain management regimes. 'Paper Pellets on a Saucer' was commissioned for *Spark* (Blue Diode Press, 2018) and uses text from Muriel Spark's novel *The Comforters* (1957). 'Unknowing' uses phrases from *The Cloud of Unknowing*. 'Girl Poets', found from reviews of female poets, was commended in the Oxford Brookes Competition 2018, and is published in the *Book of Bad Betties* (Bad Betty Press, 2021). 'Your ex-first-love is an internet guru, and this is what he says' is found from social media posts.